Para  Creatures

Investigating Cryptozoology

Conrad Bauer

Disclaimer

All rights reserved. No part of this publication or the information in it may be quoted from or reproduced in any form by means such as printing, scanning, photocopying, or otherwise without prior written permission of the copyright holder.

Disclaimer and Terms of Use: Effort has been made to ensure that the information in this book is accurate and complete. However, the author and the publisher do not warrant the accuracy of the information, text, and graphics contained within the book due to the rapidly changing nature of science, research, known and unknown facts, and internet. The author and the publisher do not hold any responsibility for errors, omissions, or contrary interpretation of the subject matter herein. This book is presented solely for motivational and informational purposes only

Contents

Disclaimer 3
Contents 5
Introduction 1
History of paranormal cryptozoology 3
Hoaxes versus reality 9
Loch Ness Monster 13
Abominable Snowman 21
Thunderbird 31
Beast of Bodmin 39
Beast of Gévaudan 49
Bunyip 57
Flying rod 65
Giant anaconda 71
Kraken 79
Reptilians 89
Wendigo 97
Conclusion 105
Further Reading 107
Photography credits 109
About the author 111
   More Books from Conrad Bauer 112

Introduction

Every culture on earth has its own tales of the paranormal. While many are stories of ghosts and supernatural events, the existence of paranormal creatures is an idea which has also spread to almost every culture. With such a vast array of differences in the world of flora and fauna, the myriad of potentially mystical creatures created by our ancestors has passed down to us. Now, we find ourselves familiar with everything from werewolves to the Tasmanian tiger. Some of these animals are flights of fancy, others are real species which have been driven to extinction. But all over the world, you will find people who are certain that they continue to exist.

In this book, we will be travelling the world and searching for the truth behind some of the planet's strangest, deadliest, and most fascinating paranormal creatures. In fact, there is a whole branch of science dedicated to the pursuit. It is named cryptozoology. The goal of cryptozoology is to peel back the curtain and discover the truth about the myths, legends, stories, and even hoaxes that exist around the world. For anyone intrigued by the natural world and the human psyche, these creatures provide a captivating history of human culture and how it differs across the planet.

From the Loch Ness Monster to the giant anaconda, there have always been rumours of something strange and deadly lurking beneath the surface of our knowledge of the natural world. Could it be possible that we have missed some of the world's strangest creatures despite them existing right in front of us? Are all of the stories simply myths and elaborate hoaxes? Is there a grain of truth to even the most outlandish stories? Read on to discover the reality behind some of the planet's strangest paranormal creatures.

History of paranormal cryptozoology

One of the first questions you might have is 'what exactly is cryptozoology?' Etymologically speaking, the word derives from Greek, translating to 'the study of hidden animals.' But it's not just the animals that lurk in the difficult-to-find places that the field concerns itself with. Instead, it is fascinated by those creatures which lurk on the edge of reality. The creatures involved – often referred to as 'cryptids' - can range from animals which are considered extinct but might have survived, all the way through to the creatures of myth and legend. As well as the cryptids more grounded in reality, we can also count those who are passed down in the form of stories and tales. It can even include those animals who are known to exist, but are documented in locations far from their usual homes, such as the folkloric big cats which lurk the English countryside. Cryptozoology exists on the fringes of science, where the paranormal crashes headlong into reality. Because of this, many traditional zoologists refuse to recognise it as a legitimate science. Due to the fleeting nature of the evidence involved, we often have to rely on anecdotes, stories, and collections to piece together anything close to the truth.

We can trace the modern version of cryptozoology back to Bernard Heuvelmans, a Belgian naturalist working in the mid-twentieth century. Heuvelmans wrote a book detailing his search for unknown animals, tracing his own interest in the subject back to a nineteenth century scientist called Anthonie Cornelis Oudemans who spent time searching for sea serpents. According to Heuvelmans, the discipline should be undertaken with a strict adherence to scientific standards, despite the difficulty in obtaining evidence on these hard-to-find animals. But with this rigour, it was important to combine a willingness to explore new possibilities, to track down the nuggets of truth in millennia of folklore. This meant that paranormal animals such as the Wendingo should be treated with the same approach as the kelpie. If we are to discover the truth that lurks behind such creatures, the search to discover the reality behind the legend is not something to be scoffed at by the traditional sciences.

Ever since the fifties, the concept of cryptozoology has become more and more ingrained in the public's minds. In addition to the growth of technology that has allowed us to investigate cryptids and paranormal activity, the explosion in international communication and the ease of access when it comes to all sorts of anthropological information means that we can compare and contrast cryptids from around the world. We can see that stories such as the Himalayan Yeti bear a great deal of resemblance to the Sasquatch of North America. Where these myths, legends, and accounts of the paranormal intersect, we can often find the grain of truth which is so essential to cryptozoology.

There are examples of animals which we had previously thought to be mere legends which have since been documented. Of all the examples, one of the best is the okapi. Before the European colonisation of Africa and before Western explorers moved into the continent to document everything they saw in the name of science, there had been rumours of an antelope which lived in the forests, an antelope with the markings of a zebra. It was dismissed as legend for many centuries until it was finally documented extensively by Henry Morton Stanley during an exploration of the Congo. After it became a confirmed new species, the okapi became the recognised symbol of the group known as the International Society of Cryptozoology. A similar tale exists about the Komodo dragon, a creature many thought to be a folkloric giant lizard. The mountain gorilla, too, was initially dismissed as being a flight of fancy. But investigation and documentation by interested parties eventually led us to discover the truth behind the legends. Finding this truth is one of the essential tenets of cryptozoology.

But that is not to say that cryptozoology is not without its critics. Due to the very nature of the subject matter, there is an increased need to rely on evidence of a dubious quality, evidence of a standard that would be rejected by most scientific disciplines. There is a determination by some of those involved in the field to pursue interests in creatures that many other scientists are sure do not exist. Because of this willingness to believe in the figures of myth and legends, many in the field open themselves up to an increased amount of influence from hoaxes and mistruths. While the majority of scientists are certain that we as humans are far from having documented every single species, they remain sure that the existence of larger undiscovered species is harder to believe. Many smaller species of beetle, for example, are discovered every year. But the potential for something as large as the Loch Ness Monster to have remained undetected for all these years is slim.

So this is where the field of cryptozoology breaks from the majority of modern science. Due to the blend of anthropology with naturalism, and with a dash of the paranormal, there is a willingness to stretch belief beyond the documented world and into the realms of faith. For cryptozoologists, there frequently is a fervent belief in the undiscovered world. Whether it is the bottom of the oceans, the middle of the bleakest deserts or the depths of the thickest jungles, there is a strong belief that the world holds more than we know. With such a wide range of creatures believed to exist somewhere in the world, finding the hidden reality within the myth is a fascinating pursuit. Because of this, the history of cryptozoology is one which lurks behind the majority of modern science. But for those who believe in the paranormal, the strange, and the undiscovered, the potential for a revelation in the world of the cryptids is beguiling and engrossing.

Hoaxes versus reality

While faith is an essential part of the nature of cryptozoology, it can have its downfalls. With so many people being so ready to believe in the existence of the paranormal and the unknown, there are many who seek to profit from their interest. The creation of hoaxes and the spreading of misinformation can cause divides in the community of cryptozoology and can cause many people to take it less seriously as a branch of science. Uncovering the truth behind many claims can be tough, especially due to the nature of the subject. The emergence of many hoaxes throughout the years has done a lot to drive the field to the fringes of academia and to lead many people to believe the practice is inherently untrustworthy.

For as long as there has been interest in the weirder creatures of the animal kingdom, there have been those who are willing to prey on people's belief in the strange and the paranormal. Our history of natural hoaxes dates back hundreds of years, with many of the more elaborate hoaxes still existing today in museums. One of history's greatest tricksters and connivers was a man named P. T. Barnum. A man swept up in the entertainment industry in the middle part of the nineteenth century, many of his stories were heightened versions of myths that he could use to titillate audiences, charging people to view his creations. One of the most famous was known as the Fiji mermaid, a gross creation he displayed with the body of the fish and an almost-human upper torso. While many in the audience were willing to believe it was true, Barnum had actually come into the possession of a mummified young monkey. Telling people he had caught the creature in the distant South Pacific oceans, he had in fact simply decorated the lower half of the creature's body with fish scales, giving it the appearance of a horrific mermaid. It proved to be a profitable creation, so he made other versions and charged the public to see them. Such is people's interest in the paranormal, that they were willing to believe that the Fiji mermaid was a real animal.

Similar hoaxes have been propagated by people such as Ray Santilli, who tricked people into believing that he had conducted an alien autopsy, and many people across North America, who have created examples of a fictional creature known as the furry trout. By coating a stuffed fish in fur, they trick tourists and the unfamiliar into believing it is a type of hairy fish found in the area. In instances such as these, there is a playfulness and a joking aspect to the hoax. But in all, they play on people's willingness to believe in the unknown and the strange that might exist beyond our range of understanding. A fine example of this comes from the English explorers who first began to document the flora and fauna in Australia. Returning to England, they told a story of a creature with the mouth of a duck, the tail of a beaver and the body of a mole. When explorers and naturalists told people in England about the creature, it was dismissed as a flight of fancy. Even when a stuffed example was brought back to England, there were those who refused to believe such a ridiculous creature could exist. As we know today, the platypus is indeed a real animal. After being documented, the platypus has moved from the world of the suspected hoax into the natural order of animal species.

Trying to determine the reality of cryptids remains a difficult venture. With many people standing to profit from their discoveries, attempting to ensure that the description of a new animal follows the correct scientific methods can be very hard. Often bouncing from fleeting descriptions to questionable evidence, those who are interested in cryptozoology must often act as detectives as well as scientists. When searching for the truth, being prepared to wade through the hoaxes in order to find the reality will become a common practice. As you become more familiar with the world of paranormal creatures, being prepared to play detective and uncover the truth can be just as rewarding as learning about the cryptids themselves.

Loch Ness Monster

Location: Loch Ness, Scotland

The first creature in this book is perhaps the most famous. The Loch Ness monster is a cryptid which has attracted the attention of zoologists and amateurs alike for centuries. In fact, our first indications that there might be something existing below the surface of the lake stem from as early as the year 565. Close to a millennium and a half later, we're still not one hundred percent sure what exactly lurks beneath the surface of Loch Ness.

Located in the Scottish highlands, Loch Ness is remote, cold, and bleak. The waters of the Loch (a Scottish word for lake) are dark and uninviting. Often, a thick, dense fog sits on top of the water and makes visibility even across the surface difficult. Below the waves, the mud, dirt, branches, and other detritus make for a maze of low visibility. Stretching twenty-two miles in one direction and just under two miles in the other, the surface area of nearly twenty-one square miles makes monitoring the lake hard. With a low population around the lake, a few villages and a castle make up the traditional home of the locals. Increasingly, there is a focus on tourism to the area as more and more people learn the legend of the monster.

The concept of a Loch Ness Monster was popularised by a man named Alex Campbell. Working as a water bailiff for the Loch, as well as writing for a local newspaper to earn a bit of extra money, Campbell first reported the account of a man named George Spicer. Spicer had been driving around the lake with his wife when the pair had encountered what they described as a 'dragon or prehistoric animal.' Spicer claimed the creature emerged from the water with another, smaller animal in its mouth. The story became a sensation. Picked up by the press, interest in the Loch Ness Monster became global. A few months later, the first possible photos of the creature followed. Now infamous, the numerous black and white images seemed to show a creature with a long crooked neck peeking out over the surface of the water. Following this, the local government moved to make the creature – whether it existed or not – a protected species. Many more accounts and alleged photos would follow and would increase the monster's fame around the world.

But this was not the first story about something lurking in the Loch. Writing in 565, an author known as Adomnán put together the Life of St Columbia, a hagiography of an earlier saint. In the text, the religious man describes watching the pagan locals bury a man who had been attacked by a creature from the Loch. The man, they said, had been swimming across the waters when the 'water beast' attacked. Saint Columbia used the opportunity to try and convert the Picts, sending one of his followers to swim in the water. Despite the beast attempting to attack the man, the sign of the cross formed by the saint was enough to ward it off. While this account could just as easily be of a walrus as that of the later reptilian monster others have described, there has long been a sense of brooding danger associated with Loch Ness.

Since the emergence of so many stories about a possible Loch Ness Monster, the desire to learn the truth has driven many people to the area. One such team arrived in 1954, when a fishing boat with sonar equipment began to report extraordinary findings. As they moved along the water, an object almost five hundred metres below began to move with them. The object was large and powerful enough to swim at the same speed as a motorised boat. After travelling with the creature for two and a half thousand feet, it vanished from the sonar detection. Many have tried to search the Loch with similar equipment since, but none have been able to lock on to the signal found in 1954.

There have been many attempts to capture the creature on film. As a modern invention, the camera has allowed us to capture paranormal phenomena on film and show it to others as proof. The problem, however, is that the medium is not infallible. With the desire to document also comes the desire to deceive. Whether purposefully or mistakenly, many of the images which purport to depict the monster have been dismissed as fakes. The most famous of these – the so-called Surgeon's Photograph – has been a bone of contention for decades. It is one of the first to show the classic idea of the creature, with the long neck and small head. For some people, the most famous of the batch of images shot that day by Robert Wilson shows the creature's head and basic physiognomy. For others, it could just as well be a piece of driftwood, an otter, a bird, or even an elephant (all of which have been suggested.) Since the mid-nineties, investigations into the photograph and its negatives have led many to believe that the photograph is an elaborate hoax, constructed using a makeshift submersible device shaped like a creature.

Other famous shots of the creature have since been declared hoaxes or fakes of one form or another. Even some attempts to capture modern video images have proven difficult. Still, however, many people travel to Loch Ness in the hope of tracking the monster down. In this respect, the best chances of documenting the creature are not likely to come from shaky tourist cameras, but rather from scientific expeditions with reliable equipment. There have been various attempts to take sonar scans of the lake, but the huge expanse of shifting water can make this difficult. Even as little as twenty-three metres below the surface, all sunlight vanishes, and at its deepest, the lake goes down ten times that far. This makes the use of submarines inefficient. One attempt to find the creature, known as Operation Deepscan, occurred in 1987 and involved twenty-four boats working in unison with echo sounder equipment to scan the lake bed. The results were inconclusive, with some pointing towards large moving objects which could have been either driftwood, seals, or the monster itself. Even the equipment owner admitted that there was likely something that was yet to be detected.

Despite the various attempts to find the truth at the bottom of Loch Ness, many people are unwilling to accept no as an answer. Because of this, many theories have come to light about what the Monster might be. One of the most popular is the idea of a plesiosaur living in the lake. Plesiosaurs were a water-dwelling reptilian species whose existence coincided with the dinosaurs. A small head, long neck and flippers fit the profile. The only problem is that they supposedly died out almost sixty-five million years ago. The Loch itself was formed only ten thousand years ago by the departure of the last ice age. Others have suggested a long-necked amphibian such as a new species of newt. Another person put forward the idea that it might be a species of pinniped (the genus containing seals) with an especially long neck.

Other people have put forward alternative suggestions for the sightings. Some could be simple cases of mistaken identity, when a drifting piece of wood seems to form the bent neck and arching back of a monstrous creature when emerging from the fog. There have been confirmed sightings of Scottish seals in the area, sometimes living in Loch Ness for months on end. While some have suggested the special breed of long-necked seal might be the origin of the stories, extant seal species could be mistaken, under certain circumstances, for something they are not. In addition to these, the possibility of a large fish such as a Greenland shark living in the waters could produce strange sonar results, with such creatures growing up to twenty feet long in similar waters. The existence of a giant eel could also lead to many of the mistaken sightings. Though they rarely emerge from the water in such a fashion, the conventional idea of a sea serpent is not strikingly dissimilar to the largest eels in the world. The appearance of two conger eels at the shore one day is believed to be a hoax, an attempt to attribute the monster's existence to giant eels living in the Loch.

The unwelcoming conditions of Loch Ness may prevent us from ever truly knowing what lives in the waters. As it stands, it seems unlikely that a creature of the size and magnitude reported could elude us for so long. But the weather conditions and the size of the Loch lead many to believe that there is certainly something strange about the waters. With so many people knowing and loving the Loch Ness monster, it has become a cultural phenomenon as much as much as a paranormal one. With books, TV shows, and films all written about the creature, its popularity remains as high as ever. Even if we never learn the truth about Loch Ness, the possibility is enough for many people to believe a strange and mysterious monster cryptid continues to hide away from prying eyes.

Abominable Snowman

Location: Nepal & Tibet

After the Loch Ness Monster, the world's most famous cryptid is probably the Abominable Snowman. Also known as the Yeti, the creature benefits from similar problems to Scotland's water creature in that the habitat where it is rumoured to live is bleak and difficult to access. The Himalayan Mountains around Tibet and Nepal do not lend themselves to curious scientific investigations into the existence of difficult-to-track creatures. Despite the cryptid's legendary status, there are some who are certain that the stories of the Yeti have some grain of truth to them. Wrapped up in local folklore and introduced into Western culture in the last two hundred years, the possibility of a giant bipedal ape wandering through the world's tallest mountain range is quite literally the stuff of legends.

Before we continue, it is important to note the main differences between the Abominable Snowman and his closest cousin, the Bigfoot or Sasquatch, which is said to inhabit North America. While both legends tell of a giant ape-like creature that exists in the wilderness, the stories of the Yeti are traced back further than those of its cousin. While the majority of evidence for the existence of Bigfoot has been discredited and the theories routinely dismissed, the scientific community remains more open to the possibility of the Yeti's existence than its New World equivalent. Rather than focus on the routinely disproved Sasquatch mythologies that have sprung up in the last hundred years, this book will choose to focus on the erstwhile tales of the Abominable Snowman.

Tracing the roots of the creatures is hard. The various groups of peoples who have made their home around the Himalayan Mountains have all ascribed a different name to the creature, as well as crediting it with different powers. In the original Tibetan, the name Yeti is a combination of 'rocky' and 'bear,' while other cultures offer up translated names in the form of 'man-bear,' 'cattle-bear,' 'wild man,' and 'snow man.' Across the region, the existence of documented animals such as the Himalayan brown bear share many of the names with the Yeti, as well as some of its qualities, such as size and power. But these cultures remain adamant that the Yeti itself is something different.

The name 'Abominable Snowman' comes to us from an English author. During an expedition into the region surrounding Mount Everest, a British soldier named Charles Howard-Bury wrote a book describing his experiences in the mountain. In the book, he mentions the discovery of a set of footprints at twenty-one thousand feet up the mountains and attributes them to a large wolf, whose four legs had exaggerated the size of each print to double its size. But his Sherpa guide had another suggestion. The guide told him the story of the 'man-bear' and told him about the existence of the creature known as 'the snowman'. When the expedition returned to Nepal, a journalist named Henry Newman interviewed them about their experiences. He was told of the snowman's traces they had encountered and there seems to have been an error in the local's use of adjectives to describe the creature. After attempting to quiz the crew about the nature of the beast, Newman settled on the phrase 'Abominable,' providing the world with the name of the mysterious cryptid that would come to be known as the Abominable Snowman.

But it would be disingenuous to suggest that the stories of the Yeti were discovered by the British. According to anthropologists, the snowman is a creature who has held a place in many of the locals' beliefs for hundreds, and possibly thousands, of years. The Yeti has variously been described by the local cultures as a God of hunting expeditions or as a creature with mystic and magical properties. Many have suggested that this large creature, shaped like an ape, carried a huge stone with him to use as a weapon, a stone which emits a whistling sound as he walks through the mountains.

Some of the earliest reports that reached Europe regarding the Yeti made reference to its ape-like qualities. Though the locals had traditionally referred to the creature as being bearlike, accounts such as that of B. H. Hodgson seem to pin the stories on an orang-utan. Any time questions were made about the existence of a giant ape in the mountains, there was little in the way of direct evidence, but only stories and accounts from the locals. Nevertheless, reports of such a creature increased during the twentieth century. As more and more westerners travelled to the region in order to attempt to scale the mountains, they took home with them the legends of the creatures known by now as the Abominable Snowmen. One member of the Royal Geographical society reports seeing a Yeti first-hand, with N. A. Tombazi's account describing a human-like figure that walked upright. When they came across its footprints, they were like those of a man but almost fifty percent larger.

Footprints such as these would cause a sensation when they were finally photographed. Eric Shipton's images of footprints at twenty thousand feet were printed around the world. Even famed climbers like Sir Edmund Hilary reported seeing these huge footprints in the snow during their Everest expeditions. Hilary's well-known comrade, the Sherpa Tenzing Norgay wrote in his autobiography that – despite never seeing a Yeti – he believed that they existed, and described them as a large creature similar to an ape. He even mentioned that his own father claimed to have seen one in the flesh.

As interest increased, there was a growth in the need for physical evidence. During the 1950s, the examination of old Tibetan artworks depicting the Yeti asserted its credentials as a local legend, while a local monastery proclaimed that they had retrieved evidence of the creature in the form of a scalp. When examined, the scalp was littered with darker hairs ranging in colour from brown to red. The scalp was sent for testing. While the results were inconclusive – the scientists could find no match against any known ape or bear – they did suggest that the hairs were unlikely to have come from a creature such as a Yeti. The number of American excursions into Nepal at this time was high enough that the US government instituted a rule for travelling citizens that they were not allowed to harm such a creature should they run into anything resembling a Yeti. While there was no evidence, the American government of the 1950s thought that the chances were high enough that the creature should form part of their foreign policy and advice to citizens.

And this is how investigations into the existence of the Yeti have continued. Throughout the decades since the news of an Abominable Snowman first broke in the west, there have been numerous calls for further investigation and many groups of scientists who venture into the wilds of the mountains to find out more. Typically, the witness accounts and the numerous footprint sightings are our greatest evidence of the creature's existence. Many of the physical pieces of evidence provided by locals is often deemed to be inconclusive or fraudulent, with some locals selling repurposed skin and hair from other animals to profit from Western tourists. We are still searching.

But how can we explain the concept of a giant ape living invisibly in one of the world's most treacherous mountain ranges? One of the most popular explanations is that witnesses are simply falsely identifying local wildlife. Creatures such as the local bears or monkeys might look – from a distance – like the Yeti. Others have suggested that these could be humans who choose to live alone out in the wilderness. But this does not account for the size of the creature witnesses have described, nor the size of the footprints. An unknown or undiscovered species of bear could be the answer, with species such as the Brown bear able to walk on two legs, reaching a huge height when doing so. But it is not a natural inhabitant of the snowy mountain tops. Similarly, the Asiatic black bear is known to spend much of its youth climbing trees, a behavior that could lead some to thinking it was an ape. Linguistic studies of the word 'Yeti' have also tried to prove that the local languages have simply altered or corrupted the traditional word for bear, changing the creature's physiognomy just as they have changed its etymology. This research has been roundly criticised, however.

Other suggestions include the idea that the Yeti might simply be an unknown population of apes that have thus far avoided scientific documentation. Species such as Gigantopithecus – though now extinct – provide an idea of what such an ape could look like, especially as the creature was an inhabitant of the regions surrounding China and India. Similarly, it could be a close, mountain-dwelling cousin of the orang-utan.

Much like the Bigfoot in North America, interest in the existence of an Abominable Snowman remains high. Unlike Bigfoot or Sasquatch, however, the existence of the Yeti is taken much more seriously by the scientific community. While it is unlikely that the creature is a hunting god or paranormal species, the idea of an ape or bear existing in the harsh region is far more likely than such a creature existing in the relatively tame environment of the American countryside. Perhaps a template for just how tough it can be to explore the regions can be found in the plight of the snow leopard. While the creature was known to science since at least the 1700s, images or film of the big cat were almost impossible to capture.

Due to the solitary lifestyle, remote location, and difficult conditions of the Himalayan leopard, it was not until the turn of the century that we managed to capture it on film. In time, maybe, we might just be able to track down similar evidence of the existence of the Yeti. Whether it is a bear, an ape, or something else entirely, we are yet to know.

Thunderbird

Location: North America

Totem pole topped by a thunderbird, Thunderbird Park, Victoria B.C.

Mythology often plays an important role in the world of cryptozoology. Before science began to answer many of the world's questions, religion, superstition, and folklore were used to help explain some of the more perturbing and confusing aspects of the world around us. While science has moved forward and our understanding of the natural world is better than ever, the remnants of these beliefs linger in our minds as legends and the paranormal. In the case of the North American Thunderbird, similar cases have been taken from across the world. Examples of giant birds are found in many cultures, but it is the North American variant that has remained a potentially viable creature and possible cryptid. While the existence of these giant birds has been a big part of Native American folklore for many centuries, it is the modern reports of undocumented avian cryptids in North America that really catch the eye.

Thunderbirds have been a part of folklore for many centuries. Giant birds such as the Roc come from Persian legends and tell us of a bird that could carry away elephants in its talons. The Phoenix is another example of a mystical bird that passed down into legend. Sometimes, these giant birds can be traced back to extinct species such as the three metre high elephant bird (hunted to extinction in the sixteenth century) and the Malagasy crowned eagle, which lived on the island of Madagascar until the 1500s. Exaggerated accounts of these creatures, as well as extant birds such as the ostrich and the cassowary could well provide the background for the old world stories. But the thunderbirds hail from another continent entirely.

Modern reports of the thunderbird are typically traced back to the late nineteenth century, when two Arizona cowboys reported spotting a bird with a massive wingspan. Rather than a conventional bird, however, their reports seemed to suggest that it had no feathers. Instead, its skin was more like that of a bat. Rather than the hooked beak of most predatory birds, the creature had a long snout, similar to a crocodile or alligator. It resembled what we might today know as a pterodactyl, a flying reptile who coexisted with the dinosaurs. While the pterodactyl was known to science, familiarity with it was not as global as many of the other dinosaurs people were more familiar with. On spotting the creature, the cowboys managed to kill it. They approached the corpse, noted its huge wingspan, and dragged the body back to the nearest town. Here, the locals pinned the creature up against a barn, stretching out the wings for all to see.

From here, the local newspaper may well have attained a picture of the creature. While we are able to trace the newspaper – the Tombstone Epitaph – and can confirm they ran a story about an unidentified winged creature in

1890, the photo has not survived. Neither has the animal's remains, and many in the area now simply chalk the story up as an urban myth. Over the ensuing decades, various people have claimed to have seen or even owned the photograph, but no such image has come to light. The account of the cowboys is impossible to verify beyond that one newspaper article.

Reports of thunderbirds then dried up for a number of years. In the 1940s, a number of different sightings were collected together by the author Loren Coleman, who writes extensively about cryptozoology. He managed to obtain a number of accounts of similar sightings from a brief window of time, all in Illinois. In 1948, a group of three people claimed to have spotted a large flying object. After initially dismissing it as a plane, they noticed that the creature appeared to be flapping a gigantic set of wings. Three weeks after this sighting, a father and son tell a story of seeing a similar giant bird, flying five hundred feet above their heads, whose shadow was similar in size to a small aircraft.

Around this time, Missouri residents began to report a number of sightings of giant birds in the area. The stories were numerous enough that the residents got together and demanded that the government do something to protect the citizens against this new threat.

The officials began to put into action a plan to catch one of the birds. On discovering a number of blue heron tracks, many of the locals were assuaged enough to believe that the giant birds were simply herons and they had been misidentified. Others were not as convinced.

One of the most vivid accounts again comes from Illinois. Three young boys were playing in the back garden of their home when two giant birds approached. While two of the boys managed to run away, the third was attacked. The ten year old was scooped up in the talons of one of the birds, its claws digging into the flesh of his shoulder. He was lifted a few feet in the air before the bird, put off by the boy's struggles, released him and flew away. Though some have dismissed the story as a fantasy and refused to believe it might be possible, others were convinced by the boy's wounds and the number of witnesses who gave similar accounts.

And accounts continue into the twenty-first century. It was 2002 when reports from Alaska described a large bird with wings stretching more than four metres across. Some have suggested that the creature might have been a large specimen of a Steller's sea eagle (native to the area) but these species typically only grow to half of the size described. As well as the reports from Alaska, people as far south as Texas have also reported the sightings of birds far larger than those typically found in the area. Added to the Native American traditions of the thunderbirds, these giant species of birds could well be an as-yet undiscovered species that exists in very small numbers across North America.

For modern cryptozoologists, the existence of such creatures is far from impossible. While ascribed many ancient powers and qualities, the folkloric thunderbirds could simply be the traditional name for a species which we have not yet encountered. A long-standing connection to stormy weather (lending the word 'thunder' to the creature's name) could well stem from the manner in which an eagle might use the air currents to fly up high, lurking close to the more boisterous weather to take advantage of the natural drafts. A man named John Keel mapped the reported sightings of thunderbirds and matched them against contemporary weather reports. He found that many sightings of the birds corresponded to the times when the storms began to move across the country.

Others have suggested that the thunderbirds could simply be an outside species that has happened to stray from its normal habitat. Rather than being a pterosaur (such as a pterodactyl) that has lived on beyond the mass extinction of its peers, it could well be a more recently extinct species of larger bird that has survived. Birds such as the Andean condor can measure up to ten feet wing tip to wing tip, while the Harpy eagle of South America can have a wingspan of seven and a half feet and is known to prey on monkeys. That a colony of these birds has moved into new territory, or may have been raised as pets and then released by careless owners, could be possible reasons why the huge birds have been spotted across North America.

The case of the thunderbirds is one where modern cryptozoology has come close to providing answers about some of the mythological, paranormal tales of old. By providing logical reasons for the existence of the strange and sensational, the field has been able to create a strong case for the existence of creatures many thought to be unreal. For those in North America, the ancient thunderbird might be far more real than imagined.

Beast of Bodmin

Location: Cornwall, England

While many of the cryptids we will encounter in this book have become globally famous creatures, there are certain entries which can be considered hyper-specific. These are limited to a particular region and are typically named after the place they inhabit. Rather than being a part of the local religion, they might exist more as a kind of ghost story. They can act as a warning and a scare tactic, something used by the local residents to worry visitors and tourists, as well as something they can tell their children. In some circumstances, there might be an element of advice wrapped up in the paranormal, the creature acting as a warning against visiting certain inhospitable areas. At other times, the creature might simply be used to drum up tourism. One of the most notorious of these creatures is the Cornish cryptid, the Beast of Bodmin.

Bodmin Moor is a wide expanse of granite moorland located in the south western county of Cornwall in the United Kingdom. The county is the farthest south it is possible to go in Great Britain, with the moor stretching right down to the tip of the cliff edges. Geologically, it is harsh and flat terrain. Unlike many rural places in the northerly parts of the country, Bodmin Moor is typically flat grassland. The granite beneath the surface of the land inhibits much from being able to grow there, leading to very little in the way of wind-breaking tree lines or copses. Mountainous, riddled with streams, and crossed with caves and valleys, the moor can be a hard place to hide when out on the large flat fields, but offers a huge number of hiding places for those who know the area well. It is not unknown for tourists, hikers, and even locals to wander around the moors and become lost. They might fall into a crevasse, twist an ankle in a hidden rabbit hole, or simply become disoriented when the fog crawls in from the sea and hinders visibility. Out of this almost-alien location, the legend of the Beast of Bodmin has sprung up.

Bodmin Moor

The Beast is what is known in cryptozoology as a phantom wild cat. Taking the appearance of a panther, a lion, a leopard, or even a tiger, these big cats and their legends are scattered across the UK and many other countries. In a nation where there are no real natural large cats, there are many legends of such animals springing up around the country. As well as Bodmin Moor, similar creatures have been described in the Cotswolds, in Inverness-shire (where a puma was caught in 1980), the Isle of Wight (where a leopard was shot in 1993), and Cricklewood (where a lynx was captured alive and placed in London Zoo.) Though there are many similar stories that have sprung up in the latter half of the Twentieth Century, there are none which have quite the same mystical qualities as the Beast of Bodmin.

What separates Bodmin's beast from the other big cat sightings in the country are the mythological qualities that are typically fused together with the scientific explanations. Firstly, the area in the south of England is often considered one of the most mythical in the country. As one of the last areas to be dominated by the Romans and with strong ties to pagan religions, the druids, and even the wizard Merlin of the King Arthur legend, there is certainly a mystical association with the county. The wild and savage nature of the terrain typically ties into this, with many people keen to relate the particular rough qualities of the Cornish countryside with a rugged form of magic. Unlike other big cat sightings around the country, the Beast of Bodmin is one of the few which arrives with a paranormal back story about its existence.

Though now forgotten, an ancient British legend revolves around the Black Dog. Hundreds of years old, the Black Dog is a spectre that travels across the British countryside, particularly around the rural areas that are less inhabited. A huge, shaggy hound, the Black Dog appears to those who are about to die. According to the legend, anyone who spots the Dog lurking around their home at night is not long for the world. A long-held association with certain areas in Cornwall meant that the legend of the Black Dog was already closely associated with the county, before taking on a hyper-specific version of the tale and becoming transformed into the Beast of Bodmin.

While sightings of such a creature can be traced back hundreds of years, it is only in the previous century that they have become specifically tied to the idea of a big cat. Throughout the many years of being retold in pubs and homes, the Beast of Bodmin has retained a few essential qualities. It is always black. Unlike other phantom big cats – which might be brown, tan, or lighter colours – the Beast of Bodmin is always described as being the darkest possible shade of black. It is very rarely seen during the day time, with the majority of the older sightings often being as simple as seeing a pair of huge glowing eyes and a deep shadow moving along the edge of a tree line, stalking the witness. Over time, what was originally a dog-like creature has become more and more cat-like. Today, many would recognise the Beast of Bodmin as something resembling a giant panther, but it has many of the qualities we might traditionally associate with the Black Dog of classic British mythology, bringing with it the same paranormal connotations as a grim spectre of death.

But unlike many of the ancient folkloric cryptids which have simply faded away as our understanding of the natural world has grown, we possess now more evidence for an actual Beast of Bodmin than we have ever done. Bodmin Moor has traditionally been a place where herdsmen graze their animals, shepherding them across the countryside throughout the day. There are often a large number of sheep spread out across a huge area at any one time. As such, there have been numerous reports of these shepherds losing members of the flock, eventually coming across the mutilated remains, their bodies torn apart by an animal of ferocious power. This is often coupled with the witness reports of those who find themselves on the moors at dusk or sunset, with their accounts often describing a huge creature prowling through the cracks in the terrain, vanishing as quickly as it appears.

Because of the on-going legend of the Beast of Bodmin and following a large spate of the mutilated sheep carcasses being found, the British government launched a probe into the existence of the phantom big cat in 1995. After returning the results of the investigation, the Ministry of Agriculture, Fisheries and Food said that they could find no evidence of such a creature's existence, but admitted that they could not prove that such a big cat was not living and surviving on the moors.

More evidence would arrive less than seven days after the report was handed in. A boy was walking through the moors near the River Fower when he came across a large skull. It appeared to belong to a big cat, but was far larger than any of the species that might be considered natural to the British Isles. The teeth were enormous and perfectly designed for chewing through flesh. The lower jaw was nowhere to be found, but the two prominent canine teeth were large enough to indicate just how much damage the creature could have done while alive. Just as the government were denying the existence of any kind of big cat on the Bodmin Moor, the skull's discovery became a huge story in the media.

The skull was sent to London's Natural History Museum for identification. It didn't take much time to confirm that it belonged to a leopard. The skull was genuine, but the museum investigators said the story did not end there. The reports indicated that while the skull really did belong to a leopard, it was not likely to have died on the moor. The evidence seemed to suggest that it had once been part of a leopard skin rug. The presence of a number of non-indigenous cockroach eggs seemed to hint that the animal had died abroad, while marks on the skull indicated that it had been skinned with a rough knife and severed from the vertebrae at a particular point. For whatever reason, someone had placed the skull on the moor to drum up interest in the existence of the Beast.

While the skull was found to be a hoax, the reports of something living on the Bodmin Moor have not ceased. For many, the legend ties in to the theory that the creature is one of any number of big cats who were once in captivity. After it became illegal to own large cats such as panthers, pumas, or lions in the United Kingdom, the owner of such an animal might have released it into the countryside. Or it might even have escaped from captivity after growing too large to be confined to a cage. The Dangerous Wild Animals Act of 1976 is often cited as the time after which many of the legends of British big cats sprang up, with owners not wanting to face prosecution for the pets they owned. Similarly, some have suggested that these isolated pockets of big cat populations are examples of big cats that survived the last ice age of ten thousand years ago.

While we might not have a definitive answer of exactly what the Beast of Bodmin is or where it came from, we do know that it is the only one of Britain's big cats to be tied to inseparably to the legend of the Black Dog. Now just as much a part of Cornish mythology as King Arthur, the Beast of Bodmin will likely survive longer than any individual escaped panther.

As long as the torn-apart sheep carcasses are being found on the moor, and as long as hikers believe they saw a dark shape prowling along a cliff's edge, there will be people who continue to believe in the existence of the Beast of Bodmin.

Beast of Gévaudan

Location: Lozère, France

Illustration of the Gévaudan beast, unknown artist, 1765

Around the world, there are a number of different cryptids that have been labelled as a 'beast.' As well as the already mentioned Beast of Bodmin, our next entry comes to us as a similar kind of story, but from an entirely different perspective. The Beast of Gévaudan (located in modern day Lozère) has been a local legend for almost three hundred years. Unlike its Bodmin equivalent, this creature does not seem to be a big cat. Instead, many have described it as a giant dog, something between a wolf, a hound, and a hyena.

Legend paints the beast as a paranormal man-eater, something which attacked and devoured locals, and something that was not of this earth. After reports of the beast's attacks began to spread around the country, the French government launched a huge hunt to track down the beast. They used the locals, trained hunters, and even the army in order to try and find the creature that was terrorising the local town. Some have suggested that the attacks numbered in the hundreds. But what exactly was the Beast of Gévaudan and where did it come from? Furthermore, where did it go?

Thanks to the literacy of the time period, and the huge fame which the beast's attacks garnered, we have a large amount of writing describing various witness accounts of what the beast looked like. Though many of the descriptions vary, the common conception seems to be that it was similar to a very large wolf. It was almost the size of a young cow and far larger than the wolves which sometimes roved through the French countryside. It was a solitary creature – unlike the pack animals that wolves are – and also possessed slightly different dimensions to most dogs and wolves. Witnesses are said to have seen short ears which jutted up straight from the creature's skull. Its chest was far larger than might have been expected, while the mouth was also larger than normal. Inside the mouth, rows of huge teeth provided a deadly collection of weapons with which the beast could attack. The witnesses describe the colour of the animal's fur as being a deep, dark red, flecked with black streaks along the body.

The first encounters with the Beast of Gévaudan indicate that the locals at the time had no idea what they were dealing with. In the summer months of 1764, a young woman saw the animal while she was taking care of her family's cows. The beast approached the herd but was driven away by the bulls as they charged the attacker down. She told friends and family members of her strange encounter, but little more could be done. A short time later, a teenager was attacked by a beast fitting the same description. The victim died, becoming the first to be attacked by what would eventually become a nationwide concern.

As the year 1764 progressed, the attacks became more and more frequent. All across the region of Gévaudan, people were being savaged, wounded, and killed by this unknown entity. Fear spread through the area. People were scared to leave home alone, especially at night. Of the reports that have passed down through the ages, we can note the particular attention the beast paid to the necks and the heads of its victims, often the first place it would attack. As incidents continued into the next year, people began to suggest that there may have even been more of the beasts, with some people giving accounts of seeing two such creatures prowling through the French countryside. Some even thought they might have seen the animal with its young, suggesting that there was a breeding population in the area.

One of the most notable encounters came when a man named Jacques Portefaix was attacked. When travelling in a group of eight people, Portefaix and his friends were set upon by the beast. They stuck together and managed to fight the animal away. But it followed and harassed them; unleashing attack after attack. Eventually, they hurt it enough to drive it away permanently. Their story became widely circulated around France, even reaching the attention of King Louis XV. The King awarded Portefaix and his friends a reward for their efforts, and indicated that the government would now step in to help find and kill the Beast of Gévaudan.

It took three weeks for the king to respond to the growing crisis. He hired two professional huntsmen - Jean Charles Marc Antoine Vaumesle d'Enneval and Jean-François, his son – and sent them to the region. They arrived in February of 1765, bringing with them the specially trained hounds they used while hunting for wolves. The father-son duo spent the next four months searching for any trace of the beast, which they believed to be a rogue group of wolves. They found nothing and the attacks continued throughout their time hunting the beast. Because of their failure, the King fired them and instead sent along his personal lieutenant of the hunt, the man who organized the royal hunting expeditions. It was June when François Antoine arrived in the region and his search continued throughout the following months. During this time, he managed to capture and kill three large grey wolves. After this, he declared that he had succeeded and that there was no possibility that there would be a wolf larger than any he had caught. Some of the survivors of the various attacks said they noticed scars along one creature's body that corresponded to places they had fought it away. The animal was stuffed and sent back to the royal court, whereupon Antoine — seemingly victorious — was awarded a large sum and treated as a hero.

But the attacks did not end there. At least twelve more deaths were reported that year, and they continued for the next few years, though not as frequently. It is thought that the beast managed to kill almost one hundred men, women, and children in all. During the time it continued to attack people, most were quick to dismiss the attacks as those of a regular wolf. They did not want to accept that the creature had come back. A local man named

Jean Chastel is said to have killed one particularly large creature close to the end of the attacks, with legend suggesting that he used a silver bullet during his hunt. This is not the only element of superstition which has been introduced to the story. But the ensuing French Revolution of the later eighteenth century distracted attention from many of the attacks, while the enlightenment gradually diminished the prevalence of superstition.

For the locals, however, the Beast of Gévaudan was always more than an ordinary wolf. Many theories abounded during the time and have continued to this day. At the time, the supernatural qualities of the beast were espoused, with the beast's amazing size and strength, as well as its ability to vanish into the night, attributed to a paranormal nature. One modern French scientist has suggested that – rather than a wolf – the beast may have in fact been a mastiff that had been bred by Jean Chastel himself, mistreated and trained to be aggressive. He even suggested that the animal might have been cloaked in a protective boar hide, preventing bullets from dealing too much damage while giving a good reason for the beast's strange colouring.

The story has traveled down through the ages and with it have come a number of stranger theories. Suggestions of werewolves terrorising the French countryside may seem to be outlandish, but the idea put forth by a History Channel documentary posited the theory that it might well have been an Asian Hyena unleashed into France by exotic animal traders. This could account for the unfamiliarity which troubled many of the victims, who would have known what a wolf looked like but might have been less familiar with a hyena. Various other media sources have suggested human involvement in some capacity, whether it was a creature bred to attack on command, and used as a weapon, or whether it was a specific breed of vicious animal that far exceeded its creator's expectations and escaped to embark on a murderous rampage. While we may never know exactly what the Beast of Gévaudan was exactly, we know the damage it managed to inflict on the French population. Far more than normal creatures, the beast's reign of terror is still remembered after three centuries.

Bunyip

Location: the waterways of Australia

Drawing of a bunyip, J. Macfarlane, 1890

For some of the world's strangest creatures – whether cryptid or not – we need only to look to Australia. With everything from the platypus to the echidna, some of the planet's strangest flora and fauna can be found on the huge island that has spent much of recent human history cut off from other cultures. This has had two effects. Firstly, the wildlife found in the country has spent much time apart from the majority of the world's other animals, meaning that their evolution has often traveled down strange and wonderful corridors. Many animals are only found in Australia, with entire groups such as marsupials being a speciality of the country. The second effect is that the local human culture is also hugely removed from what we know and expect. Influenced by the traditional stories of the native Australians, even recent folklore from the island has a specifically Australian flavour. A fine example of this is the bunyip, a very Australian cryptid.

The word 'bunyip' comes from the Aboriginal Australian languages. While there are many different equivalents from cultures around the country, including kianpraty, the word they typically refer to is 'devil' or can be translated as a kind of evil spirit. Since the arrival of the European cultures and the co-opting of the languages and stories of the native peoples, the word has since come to have new meanings. It can be used to refer to any kind of pretender, a kind of impostor, or something that is pretending to be something other than what it is. While this word has crept into the common Australian lexicon, most are aware of the strange creature that is traditionally associated with the word. As such, there have been landmarks such as rivers and towns named after the bunyip, demonstrating the extent to which the word has become commonplace in the country.

While the word itself might be popular, there is no one idea of exactly what a bunyip looks like. Instead, it seems to be a catch-all term for any kind of mysterious water creature which has evaded proper documentation. One description from the Moorundi people describes a bunyip as a type of giant, malicious starfish. As more and more naturalists began to investigate the creature, they built up a profile of the bunyip's appearance by collating as many possible versions and combining them, almost like a sketch artist might put together a criminal profile using witness accounts. What emerged was a strange animal. It was described as having a face like that of a dog, but with the head shape of a crocodile. Its body was covered in a dark fur, running across the back until it reached a horse-style tail. Its feet seem to be either flippers or webbed enough to appear so, specifically designed for use in the water. It might have tusks similar to a boar or a walrus, emerging from a flat, wide mouth. The animal seems to be almost like a platypus in some respects, but seems bigger and more aggressive. It is quite unlike anything that has been documented by science.

Attempts to explain the mythology have existed ever since westerners first came to Australia. Some have suggested that the animal is a throwback to a time when seals might have ventured inland along the coast of Australia. Their dog-like faces and fur coating seem to match the descriptions of part of the bunyip, but don't exactly fit the profile. Another suggestion is that the animal is a cultural artefact, passed down by the local peoples as a story about a now-extinct animal. It could be that the ancient peoples either encountered one of Australia's strange and unique animals and have passed down the story, or even that they came across fossilised remains and attempted to explain the creature's existence.

When the Europeans first arrived on the shores of Australia, the local's stories of bunyips seemed to prepare them for an encounter with a creature they could eventually expect to find. Just as many Europeans had never seen a koala or a kangaroo, this strange new land held many possibilities for species previously considered to be too strange to exist. The idea that there might be a larger, mammalian animal inhabiting the fresh waters certainly seemed plausible. Western accounts of bunyips emerge from the era when the newly arrived people tried to make sense of the unfamiliar habitat. That they should latch on to the local legend of the bunyip as a catch-all term for the unknown is one theory for the creature's notorious existence.

Throughout the nineteenth century there seemed to be a drive to connect the bunyip of aboriginal mythology with the wave of new creatures that the westerners were reporting back to their scientific institutions. Accounts from settlers were a common occurrence, with some people describing the creatures as being almost like a hippo or a manatee. Recent palaeontology finds in and around Australia have uncovered a creature known as the diprotodon, a now extinct breed of mammal the size of a hippo, described as a larger, water-dwelling version of a wombat. The bones of these creatures bear a striking resemblance to those of a hippo and could well be mistaken for such an animal. When shown the bones, aboriginal Australians have confirmed them as belonging to a bunyip. It could well be that the bunyip was the last remaining descendant of the diprotodon, which then became extinct, with the name being passed on to describe other kinds of similar animals, often with added mythological qualities.

Even though it seems as though the diprotodon bones provide the template for the idea of an extinct species of animals that passed down from generation to generation as a legend, that did not prevent the accounts of bunyips from continuing throughout the nineteenth century. In 1847, one man described his confusion at seeing a creature he described as a bunyip or a giant platypus. It was sunning itself on the shore of the River Yarra. After a small crowd gathered to watch, the creature vanished back into the water. Other accounts trickled into the media throughout the turn of the century, eventually drying up by the time the twentieth century arrived.

But the name of the bunyip has lived on. Now that it is a familiar part of Australian culture, most have given up hope that it could actually be a mysterious cryptid that escaped detection by the early settlers. Whether it was a case of mistaken identity, the last examples of a dying breed of ancient animals, or whether there are still a few bunyips scattered around the waterways of Australia, we may never be certain.

As an example, the bunyip is a clear indication of the extent to which people can normalise the strange and the wonderful, eventually turning what was one of the natural world's great mysteries into another name for a water spirit. Though few people search for living bunyips, there is still a quest to know exactly who, what, and why they used to be such a common part of the Australian eco-system.

Flying rod

Location: all over the world

It may seem that the majority of the cryptids we encounter in this book are larger animals, creatures whose existence should be easy to verify and who should have trouble hiding from sufficiently thorough scientific investigation. Similarly, it seems that almost all of the cryptids are associated with some form of folkloric paranormal activity. But there are cases when the creatures in question are much smaller. Rather than overlapping with the realms of magic and witchcraft, some are instead associated with the world of the extra-terrestrial. Believe in UFOs is, in many ways, the modern equivalent of a belief in magic — search for truth and reality beyond that which is conventionally accepted. Whereas we might once have attributed certain phenomena to witchcraft, we might now attribute it to an extra-terrestrial influence. In the case of rods, the phenomena has long been associated with UFOs and the influence of non-human life. These tiny cryptids have remained unexplained for many years.

Also known variously as air rods, skyfish, solar entities, or flying rods, 'rods' is often a catch-all word used to describe a strange and mysterious phenomena. Described by some as not just cryptids, but 'extra dimensional creatures,' their existence has been debated in many disciplines. They have been categorised as both miniature UFOs and tricks of the light. Their fleeting passage is hard to capture on film and they do not seem limited to a specific geographical area. Affected by the presence of insects and the presence of strong light, they are often invisible to the naked eye. It is only when we start to try and detect them using cameras that they become a visible entity.

When photographed, the rods appear as small strings of interconnected rings of light. They seem almost like a chain of particles bound together. Ranging from a few nanometres to almost a centimetre long, they vary in length but remain very small. The first filmed examples are inherently linked with the world of ufology, having been noticed in Roswell, New Mexico by a man who was attempting to film the presence of an unidentified flying object. Instead, the 1994 film captures something much smaller but no less mysterious. When playing his movie back, Jose Escamilla noticed that the small rods were swarming around the light sources in the video. With no idea what they might be, he began to ask friends. No one had an answer, and the images spread around the community. Since then, Escamilla has managed to capture more films of the little rods and has even toured across the country detailing his findings about the weird phenomena.

Some people were quick to dismiss the phenomena. Some labelled it a trick of the light or an illusion. Similar effects were created when moth wings were filmed at high exposures, their wings tracing shapes in the air that were remarkably similar to the flying rods. The fast beating of the wings created a motion blur effect that, while invisible to the naked eye, appeared to be a very strange phenomena when captured on film. But these explanations did not stop the rods from becoming a global concern. As more and more reports began to emerge from across the world of similar strange creatures, the fame and the notoriety of the flying rods reached new corners of the globe.

One of the biggest areas of interest was China. In 2005, a Chinese television network broadcast a long documentary about the rods and their appearances across China. Though various scientists were quick to debunk the rumours and explain away the emergence of the rods, images from CCTV cameras appeared to show more rods than ever before. The creators of the documentary were unable to get a firm answer on exactly what was happening and where the rods had come from. To try and solve the mystery, they laid a trap. Large nets were laid around the CCTV camera and used to trap the rods as they appeared on film. When they returned to the nets, the investigators found that there was nothing that resembled the flying rods inside. Instead, there were a large number of moths and other insects. For some, this just confirmed the theory of the beating wings on film. For others, including Jose Escamilla, the idea that the nets could capture something like the flying rods seemed preposterous. Similar stories of rods in Malaysia and other countries confirmed that the stories were not going away and that many were left unsatisfied by the explanation of the rods as simply a trick of the light.

To this day, the ufology community remains split over what exactly the flying rods are. While many people have accepted the optical illusion theory and moved on to other mysteries, there are some who remain convinced that the rods are a type of cryptid yet to be explained by science. The rods are a great example of how modern cryptids can emerge, grow, and gather together a following of believers. Whether they are simple tricks or actual creatures, there is no definitive proof.

As with many other cryptids such as the Yeti or Loch Ness monster, some people take a lack of evidence to be proof of a creature's non-existence, while others take it to mean the exact opposite. Settling on one definitive answer remains impossible until more research is carried out.

Giant anaconda

Location: throughout South America

Green anaconda

One of the most common features shared by paranormal cryptids is their enlarged size. Many of the creatures featured in this guide are defined by their outlandish size and the fact that they're so much bigger than expected. With this increase in size comes an implicit increase in the power and the threat of the animal, allowing the cryptid to prey on humans at will. Even when the creature is not obviously paranormal, there is a strangeness and an uncanniness to those animals that are far larger than we might expect. A fine example of this is the giant anaconda that has supposedly terrorised much of South America for hundreds of years. As deadly and fearsome as the normal anaconda might be, the thought that there exists a gargantuan version lurking beneath the surface of the Amazon is enough to worry most people.

For a long time, there have been legends of a giant snake being that lives in the South American rainforests. Somewhere between a god and a sea monster, figures such as Yacumama have been a part of the folklore of the indigenous peoples for as long as they can remember. Yacumama was said to be fifty feet long and was the mother of all the other animals in the world. Her home was the mouth of the Amazon River and the creature would devour any being that stepped within one hundred feet of its home. To ward off the spirits and protect those who might be venturing close to the animal's territory, the people would blow hard into a conch horn. The sound would supposedly ward off Yacumama and allow the people to pass by in peace.

The legend is not too hard to believe. Anacondas themselves are native to the whole of tropical South America and pose a big threat. As one of the world's largest snakes, they can grow up to seventeen feet long. As well as being one of the world's longest snakes, they are certainly the heaviest, with some of the larger snakes reaching up to seventy kilograms. Almost all of this is muscle, stretched out along the length of the animal's body. This makes it a powerful predator, capable of crushing the bones of its prey as it constricts itself around them. Their diet is wide reaching, spreading from smaller fish and birds, right up to deer and even crocodiles. When they come close to human farms, they can attack and kill cattle, and it is not unknown for them to indulge in cannibalism, killing and eating their own species. They are naturally water-born creatures, meaning that it is often difficult to see the entire animal before it is too late. While the small head might jut out above the water, the rest of the snake's body lurks beneath the surface, coiled and ready to strike. Even though they find it difficult to move above the water, they can still slither silently through the undergrowth. With eyes and noses that can completely close, they are capable of sitting beneath the water for extended periods of time, remaining out of sight from even a close perspective.

With such a powerful predator sharing the same habitat as the indigenous people of South and Central America, it should come as no surprise that the anaconda was treated with such reverence by the local peoples. But what about the giant anaconda's appearances to the western invaders of the seventeenth century and later?

During the European colonisation of the Americas, the colonists would frequently learn the legends of the local people. One of the most common referred to the giant anaconda of folklore. These tales suggested that the creature could reach almost one hundred and sixty five feet long, the length of an Olympic-sized swimming pool. More commonly, however, the tales of the giant anaconda would involve a creature reaching lengths of up to fifty or sixty feet. While not as long as some of the more dramatic stories, these creatures are still more than twice the size of the largest regular anacondas.

It can be hard to imagine the strangeness of the first Europeans excursions into the South American jungles. The forests are thick, sweaty and make movement very difficult. It is possible to vanish from plain view in only a few feet, with the jungle seeming to swallow people whole. This is coupled with the discovery of the world's largest river, the Amazon, whose mouth can appear to be almost the size of a small sea. These explorers soon began to encounter the anacondas. Though not usually a man eater, the size and the strength of the snake are scary enough in their own right, especially to Europeans whose snakes rarely exceed a few feet in length. As well as seeing the regular anacondas, the sightings of the giant anacondas grew more and more regular the deeper the Europeans went into the jungle. Their stories (and their fears) were confirmed by the natives, who would tell them tales about anacondas stretching to thirty feet in length.

Even many centuries later, there are still reports of giant anacondas emerging from the jungle. The stories have become so numerous that the Wildlife Conservation Society has posted a large bounty for anyone who is able to deliver a live anaconda stretching close to thirty feet. Despite many people claiming to have seen such a beast, the prize remains unclaimed since it was introduced in the 1900s. Perhaps closest was a fuel expedition undertaken in the 1940s. The group travelled deep into the jungles of Colombia and claim to have encountered an anaconda that measured almost forty feet. Unfortunately, they were unable to bring it with them when they left the jungle. A scientist named Vincent Roth claimed to have a similar story, reportedly shooting a thirty-three foot anaconda during his travels. Roth, too, was unable to provide the proof of his claims, however. An adventurer named Percy Fawcett and an historian named Mike Dash have both claimed to have seen anacondas that far exceed the expected lengths, but both have had their claims dismissed. Dash's claims seem to have held the most weight, with the historian even managing to take a few photographs before the creature vanished once again. While they photos did indeed show a giant snake, they lacked any means of judging its size, missing any point of reference that could be used to determine the creature's length.

The stories have continued into the twenty-first century. An episode of the television series River Monsters investigated the existence of the giant anaconda. The investigation brought the crew to a village where the locals confirmed that there had been a giant snake in the area recently. It had been laying in the sun, whereupon one of the locals shot at it with a gun. They failed to cause it any harm, and the snake simply slithered away into the undergrowth. The locals found three discarded lead bullets where it had been laying, seemingly as they had failed to pierce its skin. The documentary tracked down the spot where the snake had been seen. While they were unable to find the snake itself, they found the huge burrow through which it had escaped. Though unpopulated, there were remains of snake skin that had been shed all around the entrance.

While we still have not been able to find the living remains of a giant anaconda, it remains one of the cryptids which is mostly likely to be provable in the near future. It is feasible that it exists, even though its dense jungle home and ability to lurk hidden beneath even shallow water make it almost impossible to detect in the world's largest rainforest. Also of note are the extinct species that used to inhabit the area. Species such as the recently-discovered titanboa show us that snakes as long as forty-two feet once inhabited the area around Central and South America. While it has been extinct for millions of years, the skeletal remains of the titanboa provide us with an example of what the giant anaconda might look like. As we move deeper and deeper into the Amazon – as a result of deforestation and other modernisation schemes – we may be inching closer and closer to the truth about the giant anaconda.

Kraken

Location: the bottom of the ocean

Kraken Drawing by Pierre Dénys de Montfort, 1801

Mythology and folklore are often a means by which people seek to explain and normalise the inherently bizarre and strange. Before the advent of science and the better understanding of the animal world which we possess today, there was a temptation to ascribe magical, paranormal, and mystical qualities to animals which are simply out of the ordinary. Of all the locations on the planet where our understanding still struggles to penetrate, the bottom of the ocean holds the most mystery. This has been the case for hundreds of years. For centuries, many of our strangest tales of creatures and cryptids has come from sailors returning to the land with stories of mermaids and sea monsters. These could simply be mythological constructs for animals known today to be seals, manatees, walruses, or narwhals. Sailors during the age of exploration were far from the stringent biological classifiers that exist today, but they still sought to explain what they were encountering on their long and arduous voyages. One of the strangest creatures which endures to this day is the Kraken, a giant squid-like creature capable of attacking boats.

It is not hard to see how a sailor's stories might be exaggerated. In the heat of the sun, often lacking in food and fresh water, working hard and for little reward, the imagination of the crew aboard a ship would surely be at risk of becoming overactive. Coupled with this, the desire to increase the danger inherent in the stories – to add foreign, strange, and exotic qualities to anecdotes –

could result from a need to impress those back on dry land. Boastful and superstitious in equal measure, the sailors of the previous centuries have often encountered sea creatures and then related their experiences back to a disbelieving audience when they arrived home. The Kraken is a prime example of this sailor's ability to exaggerate and emphasise the qualities of creatures which are already fantastically beyond the realms of normality.

The original legend of the Kraken comes to us from the deep waters surrounding Greenland and Norway. The traditional legends are likely linked to the occasional sighting of a creature known as the giant squid, a species which can grow up to fifty feet in length. The huge size of these creatures, coupled with their fearsome appearance, makes them the perfect material for scary stories retold by returning sailors.

Our first account of such a creature comes from an Old Icelandic legend (a saga) named Örvar-Oddr. In the text, the characters are aboard a ship sailing around Greenland. During their trip, sailors aboard the boat spot two giant monsters in the sea. These are the Hafgufa (translated as 'sea mist') and Lyngbakr (the 'heather back.') Of these, scholars now believe that the sea mist – the Hafgufa – is an early version of what would later be known as the Kraken. The Lyngbakr is commonly thought to be a type of whale, while the Hafgufa is described as being bigger still and the largest monster that dwells in the seas. It is capable of attacking, destroying, and swallowing ships, as well as whales and other prey. The text describes its behavior, lurking in the depths of the ocean for days at a time. When it is ready to attack, the head begins to rise just above the sea and waits for the tide to change. In the account, the Kraken is battling a giant whale and winning. The narrator claims that both creatures have been sent to kill them by magical means.

From there, we have Old Norwegian texts that take a more scientific approach to trying to describe the giant squid creature. Konungs skuggsjá, written around 1250, gives us many details of the creature, including its appearance and its diet. For the author of the book, there could only ever be two of the creatures in existence. While sailing around the creature's habitat, only two had ever been spotted at any one time. The numbers never seemed to increase, implying that the animals were not able to reproduce. As well as this, however, he classifies the Kraken as a fish. Describing the squid-like animal as 'incredible,' the author admits that very few people have ever had the chance to look upon the creature. Again, it is referred to as the Hafgufa, with the writer describing its size as being closer to an island than a normal sea animal.

It would not be until 1735 that the writer Carolus Linnaeus would reclassify the Kraken as being a part of the cephalopod family. While he gave it a scientific name and wrote about it in his book Systema Naturae, it was later removed from the following editions of the book. Linnaeus described the creature as a 'unique monster' and admitted to having never seen it himself. Throughout the 1700s, more and more people began to include the kraken and similar creatures in their accounts of the fauna of Scandinavia. The Bishop of Bergan reiterated the idea that the animal was something more akin to an island than a typical creature, also claiming that it was able to create whirlpools and that these whirlpools were the real danger to the sailors. The bishop also adds to claims that the kraken was able to attack ships using its tentacles. According to his book Det Forste Forsorg paa Norges Naturlige Historie, the kraken could wrap its tentacles around the body of a ship and drag it down to the bottom of the ocean. There were suggestions that a similar creature had washed up on shore in Alstahaug, but the comparatively smaller size of the still huge squid led many to believe that this must be a young and careless kraken, not yet grown to its full fearsome size.

Some of the most outrageous claims about the kraken were not made until the nineteenth century. In 1802, Pierre Dénys de Montfort wrote about the various species of giant octopus. For him, there were two distinct species. The first of these was the kraken octopus, the same as had been described by the Scandinavian sailors, as well as accounts coming from the new world in North America. The second type was what he referred to as a colossal octopus, a similar though larger beast that he said had been seen near the coast of Angola. He claimed that such creatures were responsible for the disappearance of ten British ships in 1782. While the incident had occurred in mysterious circumstances, a survivor came forward to state that the loss of ships was actually down to the hurricanes in the region, causing a great deal of embarrassment for the author.

After reviewing all of these accounts, it is possible to build an image of the kraken as it was commonly held. It is chiefly a squid-like creature, the longer head and tentacles more akin to the squid than the octopus. As well as the normal tentacles covered in suckers, it is also said to possess a row of spikes along each limb. Some of the earliest accounts seem more like a giant crab than a squid.

Some accounts also blame the creature for what we now know to be volcanic activity occurring deep below the surface of the ocean. The bubbles, strange currents, and even the sudden emergence of new islands are often a result of underwater geological activity. While knowledge of such features would have been unheard of back in the time of writing, these phenomena were pinned on a creature which many of the sailors already held to be real.

While we now know that the geological activities are likely the result of the specific volcanic activity below the waves, we have also encountered creatures that bear a striking resemblance to the kraken of mythology. Though it was often dismissed as simply a myth by many scientists in ages gone by, our knowledge of the deep sea has increased exponentially in the last hundred years. As our equipment has gotten better and better at withstanding the huge pressure of the depths, we have been able to document many strange and wonderful creatures in their natural habitat. As well as this, the use of photography and preservation methods mean that any creatures that might be washed ashore or caught in nets can be documented before they rot or decompose. Thanks to these advances, we have come across two creatures that are incredibly similar to the kraken of old.

The first of these is perhaps the most famous. The giant squid is a species of cephalopod that lives deep down in the bottom of the ocean. Due to a phenomena known as deep-sea gigantism, it is able to reach sizes unheard of closer to the surface. While many squid are able to reach a length of maybe a few feet, the giant squid has a length of up to forty three feet. There have even been claims of specific giant squid reaching more than sixty six feet in length, though these are more difficult to confirm. For years, our only evidence for the existence of these creatures came from the combination of the witness accounts of old sailors and the instances where a dead animal might wash up on a shore. Taken from the immense pressures of the depths of the ocean, the animals never seemed to last long once up on the surface and this made them very difficult to study. In 2004, however, a Japanese science crew managed to capture the first images of a giant squid in its actual habitat. Since then, a number of submersibles have managed to capture video of these huge creatures as these move below the waves. Thanks to the scars and wounds we have found on sperm whales, we even know that the squid have battled whales in the past, adding extra credence to the old legends passed down to us.

But the giant squid is not alone. There is another, even more mysterious creature that might have helped form the legend of the kraken. While the giant squid is the longest cephalopod we know of, an animal named the colossal squid is actually larger. Though it has shorter tentacles than its cousin, its body is much, much larger. Similarly able to reach sizes of forty or so feet long, the colossal squid is able to weigh over sixteen hundred pounds. This makes it the largest invertebrate on earth. If we examine the legend of the kraken, we will often find people who compare their body to islands and huge landmasses. If a colossal squid reached the surface, then it would be a fearsome and strange sight, its huge eyes coming close to the top of the water to lock gazes with the observer. More likely to live in the darker, colder waters surrounding the Antarctic, we have very little provable knowledge about the species. Only two have ever been recovered and both were dead. As a powerful, strong creature, it can help us understand more about the mythical cryptid known as the kraken.

Whichever species of enormous squid you happen to believe birthed the kraken legend, there can be no doubt that the grain of truth found within the sailor's stories was more robust than many imagined. Though often dismissed, our increasing knowledge of the deep sea has meant that we are finding more and more evidence of creatures that fit the profile of animals previously dismissed by science. It is often said that we know more about the surface of the moon than we do about the very bottom of the ocean. As we continue to explore our planet, who is to say what we'll be able to find and which cryptids might find themselves suitably explained in the coming future?

Reptilians

Location: hidden among society

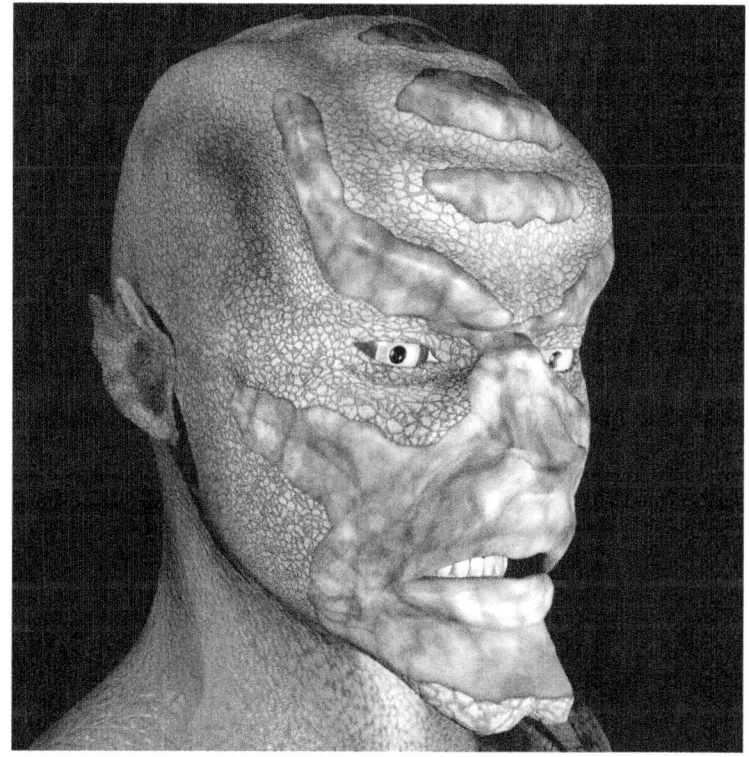
Interpretation of a reptilian

Many of the cryptids featured in this book can be traced back to a grain of truth. There might a real world template on which the creatures are based, or they might be the combination of several misidentified animals. But while we are sometimes able to retrospectively solve the mystery of how the legend of a cryptid is formed, this is not always possible. Despite the acceptance many paranormal creatures have earned from the scientific community, there will always be certain creatures that seem too outlandish to ever be accepted by the mainstream scientific and cultural community. One of the worst offenders in this regard are the Reptilians. Masquerading under a number of different names, they might also be known as Draconians, Saurians, Reptoids, or Reptiloids. Sometimes they are simply referred to as lizard people. Whichever name people choose to use, they are referring to the phenomena posited by some people that there exists a race of shape-shifting reptilian people who inhabit the earth. Disguised as humans, they move among us. For some, the mythology goes so far as to suggest that our world leaders are actually these reptilians exerting control over the planet. But where has the idea come from?

Even though a number of the cryptids featured in this book can trace their roots back to ancient societies and belief systems, the reptilians are one of the most recent additions to the world of cryptozoology. In this respect, they remain a controversial inclusion. But with the outlandish claims attributed to many other cryptids, it seems that they warrant discussion (if not belief) just as much as the Loch Ness Monster. Some have suggested that the concept of a reptilian people can be traced back to the writings of one man. The author Robert E. Howard – creator of the Conan the Barbarian series – wrote about the serpent men, a race of reptilian humans who acted as regular antagonists. Their first appearance was in his book The Shadow Kingdom and Howard is said to have based their creation on legends from Lemuria and Atlantis, lost kingdoms of ancient renown. These creatures were human shaped but with snake-like heads and scaly skin. Additionally, they possessed the ability to take on a human form at will. They were subterranean beings, living underground and plotting against humanity using mind control and shape shifting powers.

After Robert E. Howard popularised his serpent men, they made appearances in other science fiction of the early twentieth century. Among the other authors who used the idea were Clark Aston Smith and – perhaps most famously – H. P. Lovecraft. Once these reptilian peoples were included in a number of fiction works, the notion of their existence began to spread beyond the world of fiction. Maurice Doreal was one of the first non-fiction writers to mention serpent men, describing them as a lizard-like race who had bodies resembling humans, but heads in the form of a large snake. They too could take on human form at will. Doreal would use the ideas in his fiction as well as his non-fiction, helping to establish a mythology and a collection of commonly held beliefs about the race of reptilians and their intentions. In his opinion, they were determined to exert their control over the human race and take over the world.

At this point, during the 1950s and 1960s, there began to exist a crossover between those who held the traditional view of the reptilians and those who began to combine them with the growing number of stories about alien abduction. Throughout this period in the middle of the twentieth century, stories about aliens became more and more common. A type of paranormal cryptid themselves, some sought to attach the emerging idea of extra-terrestrial life with the now-established concept of a race of shape-shifting lizard people. A report made in 1967 in Nebraska involves a police officer named Herbert Schirmer who gave an account of his alien abduction. He claims that he had gotten a good look at the aliens and described them as being like a 'winged serpent,' with his descriptions bearing a large resemblance to the lizard people becoming more and more common in both fiction and non-fiction.

The idea of the reptilians gained its greatest proponent in the form of David Icke. Commonly known among conspiracy theory circles as one of the leading thinkers, Icke has helped popularise and codify the idea of the lizard men. In his detailed descriptions, they are between five and twelve feet tall and drink blood. They are able to shape-shift and have traveled to Earth from the Alpha Draconis star system. They hide on Earth in underground bases, from which they are able to exert their powers to control a worldwide conspiracy. They are anti-human and seek to take over the planet. In order to accomplish this goal, they have seized control of many of the world's leaders, including the former President George W. Bush and the Queen of England, Elizabeth II. Icke's ideas have become increasingly known – if not believed – by the mainstream media. He has had his works published in almost fifty countries around the world, and often gives lectures to crowds of up to six thousand people. In a poll taken of Americans in 2013, it was found that as many as four percent of people believed in the ideas put forward by David Icke. For a fringe conspiracy theory involving the takeover of the planet by a race of reptilian cryptids, this number is far higher than many expected.

Unlike the other entries in this book, the idea of the reptilians is inseparably linked to the world of politics. Thanks to writers such as David Icke, the existence of the reptilians is now no longer a matter just for cryptozoologists. Instead, it is a global conspiracy theory with huge ramifications should it be proven to be true. As the idea has become more and more widely known –

especially thanks to the growth of the internet – the idea has been more commonly discussed. Since the turn of the millennium, more and more people have become interested in the idea that the politicians of the world might be reptilians in disguise. In order to find evidence of those who might be involved, people have trawled through the world of politics.

While evidence has been scant and is typically based on conjecture and guesswork, one of the primary pieces of material put forward comes from March 2013. A video taken from the 4th of March depicts one of President Obama's security detail who possesses a number of unusual features. The images were seized upon and spread around the web. For some, this was the veil of shape shifting reptilians slipping, if just for a second. Even mainstream publications such as Wired posted a report about the video, admittedly with a tongue in cheek approach. It even included a quote from the NSC spokeswoman, who joked about plans to replace the President with a robot or alien. Despite the ridicule the concept received in the press, there were those who took the image to be another part of the proof needed that reptilians are among us.

As one of the stranger entries in this book, it is probably no coincidence that the idea of the reptilians is also the youngest cryptid we have discussed. While the other paranormal animals have had hundreds of years to become normalised elements of our mythology, the reptilians are still fresh in our minds. We are able to trace their existence from the first fictional accounts, to the desperate searching for evidence to prove a conspiracy theory. Perhaps because of this, they are among the first cryptids to be ridiculed. Even though most believe their existence to be preposterous, the evolution of a brand new cryptid is certainly interesting in its own right.

Wendigo

Location: Atlantic Coast of North America

The final entry into this book travels back to North America. Here, we find a breed of cryptid that has not only become a local legend, but that has passed into the medical lexicon to represent a mental health disorder that is recognised across the planet. While most paranormal creatures can trace their roots back to ancient species or incorrectly identified animals, the wendingo of North America might just be the best example of a type of human behavior that has been reclassified as a myth. Without our improved understanding of mental health and psychology, our forebears sought to explain mental health conditions in a variety of ways. The more extreme the condition, the more extreme the explanation. In the case of human cannibalism, the affected people would need an incredibly strange explanation for what compelled them to eat the flesh of a fellow man.

The legend of the wendingo comes down to us from the Native American populations along the West Coast of North America. Among those who are known to tell similar stories are the Cree, the Ojibwe, the Saulteaux and the Naskapi, as well as others. Though the descriptions of the creatures vary slightly, there is one common feature among all of those affected: the desire to eat human flesh. In all of the cultures, wendingos are aggressive, paranormal, and cannibalistic. They have a number of associations, including the cold, harsh winters found in the north of the continent and the plight of starvation and famine that could sometimes beset these people.

In searching for a description of a wendingo, one of the best descriptions comes to us from an Ojibwe man named Basil Johnston. He said that the wendingo would be an incredibly skinny and malnourished creature. It would be gaunt, with skin pulled tight across its visible bones. The skin transformed colour, turning grey and ashen, while the eyes were pushed further and further back into the skull. It looked like a creature recently risen from the dead. Lips would be shredded and covered in blood, with the whole creature covered in various open wounds. At all times, the wendingo smelled like death. Added to this, we understand that the wendingo would be a greedy and gluttonous killer. Never satisfied to kill and eat just one person, they would constantly be prowling around looking for more violence to inflict and more flesh to eat. For certain cultures, the myth of the wendingo acted as a warning against selfishness. It was the fate of those who refused to share. For these cultures, it helped to encourage people to cooperate.

In the legends of their frightening appearance, wendingos were said to be quite a bit taller than humans. While certain cultures debated the size, they ranged from slightly larger than people to many times their size, almost like giants. The flesh that a wendingo ate from a person would allow it to grow, raising up to a height equivalent to the amount of meat it just devoured. This meant that the creature could never be really satisfied and was always searching for a next meal.

Because of this, the wendingo is able to represent both starvation and gluttony at the same time.

Perhaps key to the mythology of the wendingo is the idea that any human was able to transform into the creature, given the right circumstances. There were two ways of being changed. Either a person ate the flesh of another human, or they were possessed by the spirit of a demonic wendingo. In times of extreme famine or difficulty, the prospect of resorting to cannibalism was warded off by the possibility that it might turn the eater into one of these cursed creatures. While not a taboo in all Native American tribes, the idea of cannibalism was forbidden in all those tribes who told the story of the wendingo. As such, the mythology acted as a form of prevention, helping ensure that various members of the different cultures avoided resorting to cannibalism. Even when times got hard and people were affected by famine, there was the spectre of the wendingo as a warning. The Cree and the Ojibwe enacted a ceremony at such times, performing rituals to ward off the wendingos and to remind people of the dangers of cannibalism.

While the history and the mythology of the wendingo has since been well documented, it is widely accepted that the legends were apocryphal. They acted as a warning against turning on other members of the cultural group and helped prevent the outbreak of cannibalism at difficult times. However, the idea of the wendingo goes deeper than that. There is now a belief in something called the 'wendingo psychosis.' This is a mental health condition in which the affected person suddenly develops an insatiable craving to eat the flesh of another person. This is the case even when there are other sources of nutrition available. Regardless of the food put before the person, they will feel the need to consume human flesh. The condition seems to be particularly threatening to those cultures who propagated the wendingo myth, an example of a culture-bound syndrome. This suggests that the folkloric beliefs and worries about cannibalism were capable of manifesting in the form of an outbreak of a little understood mental health condition.

The awareness of the wendingo myth meant that those in the cultures of the Native Americans along the west coast were particularly at risk of falling to the wendingo psychosis. Their genuine belief in the existence of wendingos meant that – should they feel themselves turning into such a creature and craving human flesh – they might often request someone to euthanize them before it was too late. Not wanting to succumb to their uncontrollable urges once they had transformed, they thought it better than they be killed rather than harm anyone. There were a number of medical and healing practices used by the local people to stop the turn. Should these fail and the person became violent (a rare occurrence,) they were executed.

One particularly vivid tale occurred in 1878. A member of the Cree people named Swift Runner lived with his family in Alberta. During one particularly harsh winter, the family were starving. The hunger got so bad as to cause the death of the first born son. Located more than twenty miles from the nearest food supply and unable to reach it in time, Swift Runner turned on his family. He killed them all and ate their flesh. The fact that he was not too far from food and that he killed every family member rather than enough for survival has led people to decide that this was not an example of a man turning to cannibalism as a last resort. Instead, he was suffering from the wendingo psychosis. When the authorities caught up with him, he was tried and executed as a murderer.

Rather than being a cryptid, the wendingo might simply be a transformation process that affects the mental health of certain people. Rather than being a different species, these are people who believe so much in the mythology of the wendingo that they believe themselves to be transforming into their worst nightmares. Given the extreme situations of the people driven to cannibalism, the emaciated bodies and open wounds that people attribute to the wendingos could simply refer to the awful situations of people in the most hazardous and life threatening conditions. Once the need to resort to cannibalism overcomes the sufferer, they become delusional, violent, and aggressive. As such, the wendingo is a real threat. Rather than being a supernatural being, they are instead human beings driven to their violent extremes by the most horrific experiences. As a means of explaining this behavior, the Native American peoples developed the mythology of the wendingo, in turn further ingraining the threat in the culture and the belief system. Unlike other entries in this book, the wendingo is not explained by looking further into the dark corners of the earth. Instead, we will find the answer when we examine the intricacies of the darkest corners of the human condition. As a cryptid, the real identity of the wendingo is not some long-lost species. Instead, it is simply a person affected by a little understood and horribly damning mental health condition.

Conclusion

Cryptozoology is a growing field. As the interest in the variety of legends and paranormal animals grows and grows, we encounter new cultures with new cryptids. Not only are these animals sometimes strange and terrifying, but they are sometimes strikingly similar to extant legends and even animals we know to have existed at one time. All of this feeds into our need for the truth. Even in the strangest of circumstances, we want to know the truth about some of the world's strangest animals.

Included below is a further reading list. The sheer number of cryptids around the world is huge. As such, there are many that we have not been able to cover in this book but are just as interesting. If you would like to learn more about the processes of cryptozoology and the rigorous methods that are used to find the truth, then it is highly recommended that you take a look through some of these books.

As we have seen, the field of cryptozoology takes into account some of the strangest, oldest, most bizarre, and even most recent examples of legends, stories, and mythologies. These are often paranormal and always interesting. As with everything in the world of cryptozoology, there are always new questions to ask and always new answers to uncover.

Further Reading

Arment, C. (2006). *Cryptozoology and the investigation of lesser-known mystery animals.* Landisville, Pa.: Coachwhip Publications.

Budd, D. (2010). *The Weiser field guide to cryptozoology.* San Francisco, CA: Weiser Books.

Coghlan, R. (2004). *Dictionary of cryptozoology.* Bangor, Northern Ireland: Xiphos Books.

Coleman, L. (2002). *Tom Slick.* Fresno, Calif.: Craven Street Books.

Coleman, L. and Clark, J. (1999). *Cryptozoology A to Z.* New York, NY: Simon & Schuster.

Conway, J., Kosemen, C. and Naish, D. (2013). *Cryptozoologicon.* [S.l.]: Irregular Books.

Eberhart, G. and Downes, J. (n.d.). *Mysterious creatures.*

Eberhart, G. and Downes, J. (n.d.). *Mysterious creatures.*

Newton, M. (2005). *Encyclopedia of cryptozoology*. Jefferson, N.C.: McFarland.

Shuker, K. (2013). *Mirabilis*. [Place of publication not identified]: Anomalist Books.

Photography credits

Abominable snowman

"Yetiscalp" by Nmnogueira at en.wikipedia. Licensed under CC BY-SA 2.5 via Wikimedia Commons - https://commons.wikimedia.org/wiki/File:Yetiscalp.JPG#/media/File:Yetiscalp.JPG

Beast of Bodmin

Beast of Bodmin

"A walk on Bodmin Moor, Cornwall (7), 30 Sept. 2010 - Flickr - PhillipC" by Phillip Capper from Wellington, New Zealand - A walk on Bodmin Moor, Cornwall (7), 30 Sept. 2010. Licensed under CC BY 2.0 via Wikimedia Commons - https://commons.wikimedia.org/wiki/File:A_walk_on_Bodmin_Moor,_Cornwall_(7),_30_Sept._2010_-_Flickr_-_PhillipC.jpg#/media/File:A_walk_on_Bodmin_Moor,_Cornwall_(7),_30_Sept._2010_-_Flickr_-_PhillipC.jpg

Besat ofGévaudan

By "AF" [Public domain], via Wikimedia Commons

Bunyip

"Bunyip 1890" by Macfarlane, J. - http://www.slv.vic.gov.au/miscpics/0/0/6/doc/mp006089.shtml. Licensed under Public Domain via Wikimedia Commons - https://commons.wikimedia.org/wiki/File:Bunyip_1890.jpg#/media/File:Bunyip_1890.jpg

Kraken

"Colossal octopus by Pierre Denys de Montfort" by en:Pierre Denys de Montfort († 1820) - from en:Image:Colossal octopus by Pierre Denys de Montfort.jpg where it was uploaded by en:user:Salleman.. Licensed under Public Domain via Wikimedia Commons - https://commons.wikimedia.org/wiki/File:Colossal_octopus_by_Pierre_Denys_de_Montfort.jpg#/media/File:Colossal_octopus_by_Pierre_Denys_de_Montfort.jpg

Wendigo

https://www.flickr.com/photos/doctorserone/4438753702/ Photographed by Andrés Álvarez Iglesias's photostream, March 2010 Creative commons public

About the author

Conrad Bauer is passionate about everything paranormal, mysterious, and terrifying. It comes from his childhood and the famous stories his grandfather used to tell the family during summer vacation camping trips. He vividly remembers his grandfather sitting around the fire with new stories to tell everyone who would gather around and listen. His favorites were about the paranormal, including ghost stories, haunted houses, strange places, and paranormal occurrences.

Bauer is an adventurous traveller who has gone to many places in search of the unexplained and paranormal. He has been researching the paranormal and what scares people for more than four decades. He has accumulated a solid expertise and knowledge that he now shares through his books with his readers and followers.

Conrad, now retired, lives in the countryside in Ireland with his wife and two dogs.

More Books from Conrad Bauer

Printed in Great Britain
by Amazon